The WORLD'S BEST **SCOTTISH** JOKES

Thanks Bill
Hazel

In this series:

The World's Best Dirty Jokes
More of the World's Best Dirty Jokes
Still More of the World's Best Dirty Jokes
The World's Best Irish Jokes
More of the World's Best Irish Jokes
The World's Best Jewish Jokes
More of the World's Best Jewish Jokes
The Worlds' Best Doctor Jokes
More of the World's Best Doctor Jokes
The World's Best Dirty Stories
The World's Best Dirty Limericks
The World's Best Dirty Songs
The World's Best Aussie Jokes
The World's Best Catholic Jokes
The World's Best Mother-In-Law Jokes
The World's Best Russian Jokes
The World's Best Fishing Jokes
The World's Best Salesman Jokes
The World's Best Computer Jokes
The World's Best Scottish Jokes
The World's Best Cricket Jokes
The World's Best Golf Jokes
The World's Best Maggie Thatcher Jokes
The World's Best Lawyer Jokes
The World's Best Business Jokes
The World's Best Holiday Jokes

The WORLD'S BEST SCOTTISH JOKES

Des MacHale

Illustrated by Graham Thompson

ANGUS & ROBERTSON PUBLISHERS

*Unit 4, Eden Park, 31 Waterloo Road,
North Ryde, NSW, Australia 2113, and
16 Golden Square, London W1R 4BN,
United Kingdom*

*First published in Australia by
Angus & Robertson Publishers in 1988
First published in the United Kingdom by
Angus & Robertson (UK) in 1988
Reprinted 1988 (twice), 1989*

British Library Cataloguing in Publication Data.

*MacHale, Des
World's best Scottish jokes
I. Title
828'.91402
ISBN 0 207 15805 3*

Typeset in Linotron Palatino

*Printed in the United Kingdom by
BPCC Hazell Books Ltd*

Jock visited London for his annual holiday and stayed at a large hotel. However, he didn't feel that the natives were very friendly.

'At three o'clock every morning,' he told a friend, 'they hammered on my bedroom door, on the walls, even on the floor and ceiling. Sometimes they hammered so loudly I could hardly hear myself playing the bagpipes.'

* * *

A little Scottish boy burst into the house and said to his father: 'Daddy, Daddy, I ran home behind the bus and saved ten pence.'

His father replied, 'You could have done better son. You could have run home behind a taxi and saved fifty.'

* * *

Scottish preacher to his congregation: 'I don't mind your putting buttons in the collection plate, but please provide your own buttons and don't pull them off the church cushions.'

* * *

Jock's wife Maggie went to the doctor complaining of pains in the stomach. The doctor told her it was 'just wind'.

'Just wind?' she screamed at him. 'It was just wind that blew down the Tay Bridge!'

Scotland is noted for its close family ties. Jock was one of nine children and when his wife died after forty years of marriage he never shed a tear. He explained to his friends – it wasn't as if she was a blood relation.

* * *

An English silver expert travelling in Scotland was asked if he would like to look at the trophies won by the Scottish national football team. He said he wasn't interested in antiques.

* * *

There are many theories about the bagpipes, otherwise known as the missing link between music and noise.

Some say they were invented by a Scotsman who trod on his cat and liked the noise.

Others claim that they are based on the noise made by a dying octopus.

However, the truth is that they were given to the Scots by the Irish as a joke – but the Scots haven't seen the joke yet.

* * *

There's a great demand for thimbles in Scotland. The Scots use them for standing each other whisky.

The king of Greenland lay dying, suffering from a complaint which baffled doctors who had come from far and wide to cure him. Finally one of them discovered what was the matter with him – he needed an immediate blood transfusion. Then another problem arose because the king had an extremely rare blood group. An international team of doctors was set up and every corner of the globe was searched for a suitable blood donor. It turned out there was only one man in the world with the same blood group as the king – a strapping Highlander now living in Dundee. He was willing and able to donate several pints of blood and the king soon recovered. He was so grateful that he sent the Scotsman a cheque for £5000.

About a year later the king fell ill again and the Scotsman was glad to oblige with enough blood to help the king recover. This time the king sent the Scot a cheque for £1000.

Soon afterwards the king fell ill a third time and once again the Scotsman was called upon. He gave the king enough blood to recover and live to a healthy old age. This time the king sent the Scot a thank-you note.

* * *

Did you hear that McDougal died of starvation?

He could not bear to eat because he had paid fifteen pounds to have his teeth cleaned.

In a fit of Christmas spirit Sandy sent Jock a Christmas present – a homing pigeon.

* * *

Jock used to give his chickens the finest whisky to drink.

He thought they might lay Scotch eggs.

* * *

A Scotsman will never be insulted if you offer him a small glass of whisky – he will merely swallow the insult.

* * *

Another Scottish preacher is said to have prayed thus after a particularly unproductive collection: 'We thank you Lord that the plate was returned safely.'

* * *

McTavish is one of the top contenders for Meanest Scotsman of the Year. A few days ago he gave each of his four children a tenpenny piece and told them to look after their money carefully. That night when they were asleep he extracted the money from their pockets and next morning whipped them for losing it.

How do you torture a Scotsman?

Nail his feet to the floor and play a Jimmy Shand record.

* * *

Jock (anxiously): 'You'll have to help me Doctor McTavish, I can't stop stealing things.'

Dr McTavish: 'Take two of these pills after meals.'

Jock: 'What happens if they don't work?'

Dr McTavish: 'Get me a crate of Scotch.'

* * *

Jock was in London wearing his tartans when a curious lady asked him if there was anything worn under the kilt.

'No, madam,' he replied with a flourish. 'Everything is in perfect working order.'

* * *

McTavish was dying so he asked if a pipe could be allowed into his hospital ward so he could hear the bagpipes for the last time.

McTavish recovered, but every other patient in the ward died.

* * *

Have you heard about the Scottish kamikaze pilot?

He crashed his plane in his brother's scrapyard.

McTavish committed suicide because he saw a cut price funeral advertised for fifty pounds and decided he had better die before he spent his money on something foolish.

* * *

Two Scotsmen, both a little the worse for drink, were talking in a railway carriage.

'Nationalization of the railways,' said one to the other, 'was the best thing that ever happened.'

'I agree,' said the other. 'You're going to London and I'm going to Glasgow and we're both on the same train.'

* * *

How did the Grand Canyon come about?

A Scotsman lost a sixpence.

* * *

McTavish has developed an ingenious method of getting free taxi rides at night. As soon as he nears his destination he asks the driver to stop so that he can go into a shop and buy some matches to search for a ten pound note that he has dropped on the floor. When he comes out of the shop he invariably finds that the taxi driver has departed and forgotten to ask for payment.

Jock arrived at the gates of Heaven and demanded admission.

'Where are you from?' asked St Peter.

'Scotland,' said Jock proudly.

'Away with you,' said St Peter. 'We couldn't possibly cook haggis for one!'

* * *

An American was hopelessly lost in the Highlands and wandered about for nearly a week. Finally, on the seventh day he met a kilted inhabitant.

'Thank Heavens I've met somebody,' he cried. 'I've been lost for the last week.'

'Is there a reward out for ye?' asked the Scotsman.

'No,' said the American.

'Then I'm afraid ye're still lost.'

* * *

There was a long queue to buy tickets for the film *The Great Miracle*. A fellow who had waited patiently for about an hour was next in line to a Scotsman who had just reached the box office.

'I'll have two of the most expensive seats available,' said the Scot, throwing down a ten pound note, 'and keep the change.' The Scot picked up his tickets and he and his wife went into the cinema.

'And how many tickets do you want, sir?' the girl asked the fellow.

'None,' he replied, 'I've just seen the show.'

Jock was out of cigarettes so he decided to ask his friend Sandy for a match. When he had got the match he searched his pockets and said, 'I seem to have forgotten my cigarettes.'

'In that case you won't be needing the match,' replied Sandy.

* * *

McDougal, surprisingly, always travelled first class on the railways. It was the only way he could avoid meeting all his creditors.

* * *

Have you heard about the Scotsman who gave a waiter a tip?

The horse lost.

* * *

An Irishman was being tried for being drunk and disorderly. The judge asked him where he had bought all the liquor.

'I didn't buy it, Your Honour,' said the Irishman. 'A Scotsman gave it to me.'

'Fourteen days for perjury,' said the judge.

Jock was on his way home late one night when a neighbour beckoned him for help. 'Here,' he said, 'give me a hand to get this pig out of the van.'

When they had got the pig out of the van, the neighbour said, 'Hold the pig still while I open the front door.'

Jock did as he was told and the neighbour said, 'Now help me to push the animal upstairs.' Jock did that.

'Now,' said the neighbour, 'help me put the pig in the bath.'

After a great deal of effort they managed to put the huge pig in the bath.

'Look,' said Jock, 'what is going on? Why the hell do you need to put a bloody great pig in the bath?'

'I suppose you're entitled to an explanation,' said the neighbour.

'You see the trouble is with my wife – she's one of those women who always know everything. If I tell her that Rangers have just signed a new manager, she says, "I know". If I tell her that a new oil field has just been discovered off the Scottish coast she says, "I know", and if I tell her that the Financial Times Share Index is likely to drop ten points over the next month she says, "I know".'

'But how is a pig in the bath going to help?' asked Jock.

'Well, tomorrow morning,' said the neighbour, 'she's going to go into the bathroom and then rush back into the bedroom and scream at me, "There's a dirty great pig in the bath", and I'm going to lie back and say to her, "I know, I know".'

Have you heard about the famous sign on a Scottish golf course?

MEMBERS WILL REFRAIN FROM PICKING UP LOST BALLS UNTIL THEY HAVE STOPPED ROLLING

* * *

A suitor was looking for Jock's daughter's hand in marriage. Jock asked him, 'Would you still marry my daughter if she had no money?'

'Yes I would, sir!' replied the poor lad eagerly.

'Then away with you,' said Jock. 'There are enough fools in the family already.'

* * *

Why are so many Scottish churches circular?

So nobody can hide in the corners during the collection.

* * *

Hamish wrote to his friend Jock: 'Why don't you write to me? You can fill your pen at the Post Office.'

After some time Jock wrote but addressed the letter to himself putting Hamish's name on the back. Then he posted the letter without a stamp. In due course it was delivered to himself but he refused to accept it. It was of course returned to Hamish whose name was on the back.

An English Cabinet minister was addressing a political meeting in Scotland. 'I was born an Englishman,' he declared, 'I have lived all my life an Englishman, and I will die an Englishman.'

'Hoots, mon,' shouted a voice from the crowd. 'Have ye noo ambition?'

* * *

The Scottish minister was in full flight on one of his hell-fire and brimstone sermons. 'When the Day of Judgement comes,' he thundered, 'there will be weeping and gnashing of teeth.'

'What about me?' interrupted one of his congregation. 'I've lost all my teeth.'

Roared the minister, 'Teeth will be provided.'

* * *

In Scotland, during outbreaks of fever, people are very careful about their drinking water. First they filter it, then they boil it, and finally they treat it with quicklime. Then, just to be on the safe side, they drink whisky.

* * *

An Englishman was boasting that some of his ancestors had been in the ark with Noah.

'At the time of the Flood,' retorted the Scot, 'we, the MacPhersons, had our own boat.'

Wedding guest: 'I believe that this is your third daughter to get married.'

McTavish: 'Yes, and the confetti is getting very dirty.'

* * *

Jock used to say that he was a grand judge of a glass of whisky – and a merciless executioner.

* * *

McDougal, while visiting London, lost a ten pence piece so he at once informed the police. Later, when he returned to the police station to inquire if there was any news of his money, he saw that the street was dug up for the laying of a new water main. 'My, but they are thorough in this city,' he said.

* * *

A Scotsman sent the following letter to a newspaper:

Dear Sir,

If you print any more jokes about my fellow countrymen, I shall cease borrowing your newspaper.

Yours faithfully,
Jock McTavish

Jock and his wife went to London by train for a weekend. There was a notice in the carriage which said:

SPITTING STRICTLY FORBIDDEN. PENALTY £5.

After a bit Jock's wife began to feel funny and said, 'Oh Jock, I think I'm going to be sick.'

'Not here, woman,' said Jock. 'It costs five pounds just to spit.'

* * *

Jock's wife arrived home with the day's provisions – six bottles of whisky and half a loaf.

Jock shouted at her angrily: 'What in the Lord's name did you bring all that bread for, woman?'

* * *

McNab's little boy entered a Glasgow sweetshop and threw a two pence piece on the counter.

'Give me one pence worth of sweet scraps and one pence back,' he said to the girl behind the counter. 'I've just had a row with my mother and I don't care what I spend my money on.'

* * *

McDougal was once guilty of false economy.

He and his wife went to bed early to save electricity, but the result was that his wife had twins.

The elders of the kirk were scathing in their description of the first sermon by the new minister. As one of them put it: 'In the first place, the sermon was read. In the second place it wasna well read. And in the third place, it wasna worth reading.'

* * *

McNab went into a barber's shop and asked the barber how much a haircut was.

'A pound,' said the barber.

'How much is a shave?' asked McNab.

'Fifty pence,' said the barber.

'Shave my head,' said McNab.

* * *

A Scottish newspaper carried the following ad in its Lost and Found columns: 'Lost – a £5 note. Sentimental value.'

* * *

McNab was travelling by train seated next to a stern-faced clergyman. As McNab pulled out a bottle of whisky from his pocket the clergyman looked at him and said reprovingly, 'Look here, I am sixty-five years old and I have never tasted whisky in my life.'

'Don't worry,' smiled McNab as he poured himself a dram. 'You're not going to start now.'

McNab decided to get married, so one morning he sent telegrams to three of his girlfriends, proposing marriage. Two 'phoned to say 'yes' immediately, and the third 'phoned that night to say the same. He married the third girl saying, 'The lass for me is the one who waits for night rates.'

* * *

How do you take a census in Scotland?

Throw a penny in the street.

* * *

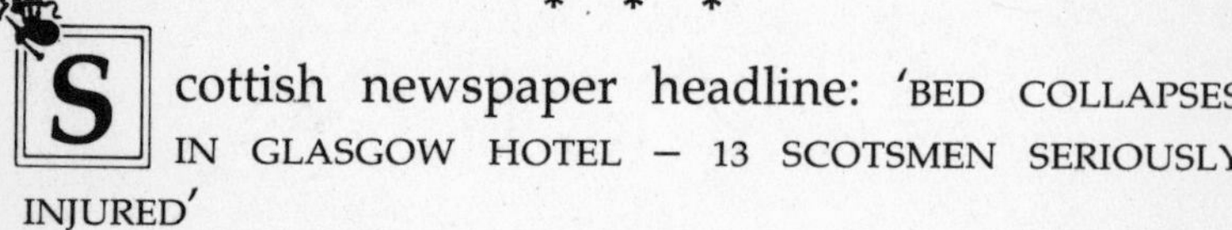

Scottish newspaper headline: 'BED COLLAPSES IN GLASGOW HOTEL – 13 SCOTSMEN SERIOUSLY INJURED'

* * *

Irate golfer, on his way to a round of 150: 'You must be the worst caddie in the world.'

Scottish caddie: 'That would be too much of a coincidence, sir.'

* * *

'I hear Maggie and yourself have settled your difficulties and decided to get married after all,' Jock said to Sandy.

'That's right,' said Sandy, 'Maggie had put on so much weight that we couldn't get the engagement ring off her finger.'

Have you heard about the two Scottish burglars who were arrested after a smash and grab raid?

They were caught when they came back for the brick.

* * *

McTavish always signs his name 'Xerxes' when sending telegrams to his girlfriend. In that way he gets two kisses on the telegram free.

* * *

McNab: 'How do you like your new radio, Jock?'

'McDougal: 'Och, it's grand, but the wee light is hard to read by.'

* * *

A Scotsman had been presented with a bottle of fine old Scotch whisky which he placed in his overcoat pocket. On his way home he stumbled and fell and as he got up he felt a wet patch on his trousers.

'Please, Lord,' he prayed, 'let that be blood.'

* * *

Why are there so few opticians and so many dentists in Scotland?

A person has only two eyes, but thirty-two teeth.

A Scottish preacher was telling his congregation about the fate of lost souls on the Day of Judgement.

'And the damned,' he thundered, 'will look on the face of the Lord and say to Him, "Lord, we didna ken." And the Lord will look down in his infinite mercy and say, "Well, ye ken the noo."'

* * *

'Just to think of it,' said McDougal to McNab. 'Poor McTavish went fishing, fell into the lake, and was drowned.'

'Are you sure he's dead?' asked McNab.

'Oh, he's dead right enough,' said McDougal. 'They fished him out, went through his pockets and he didn't even move.'

* * *

Jock had a problem with gambling and made many unsuccessful attempts to give it up. When his wife told him that he couldn't give it up no matter how hard he tried, he said to her, 'Wanna bet?'

* * *

Englishman: 'In Scotland, the men eat oatmeal; here in England we feed it to our horses.'

Scotsman: 'That's why English horses and Scottish men are the finest in the world!'

McNab came across an overturned car at a level crossing. Beside the car lay a man covered in blood and moaning.

'Did you have an accident?' asked McNab, who was noted for his powers of perception.

'Yes,' groaned the man. 'Get a doctor quickly.'

'Have the police and insurance people arrived?'

'No, no,' groaned the man, 'please get me a doctor.'

'Move over, man, and let me lie down beside you,' said McNab.

* * *

McTavish was on his way home from the pub one night when he came across a little boy sitting in the gutter, crying furiously.

'What's the matter, wee laddie?' he asked.

'I've lost my penny,' wailed the little lad.

'Don't cry, here's a match to find it with,' said McTavish.

* * *

In a village near Inverness there was a Scottish lad of fourteen noted for his innocence and simplicity. The lad's name was Sandy McPherson. For the amusement of tourists, the locals would play the following trick on him time and time again. They would offer him the choice between a shiny new fifty pence piece and a battered old five pound note. On every occasion he would ponder and ponder and

after a lot of hesitation would always choose the shiny new fifty pence piece. After some time he became a tourist attraction and busloads of visitors would stop to laugh as they watched Sandy in action.

Finally the local schoolmaster took him aside and said to him, 'Sandy, you're a big lad now, and I hate to see you being made a fool of by all these foreigners. I have to tell you that a five pound note, even a battered one, is ten times more valuable than a fifty pence piece, no matter how shiny it is.'

'Och, I ken that very well,' said Sandy, 'but if I ever chose the five pound note, nobody would offer me the fifty pence piece again.'

* * *

From the For Sale columns of a Scottish newspaper: 'For sale – secondhand tombstone, going cheap. Great value for anybody named McTavish. Owner going abroad.'

* * *

Two Scotsmen had just arrived by rail in London from Aberdeen.

'That was a long and exhausting journey,' said one.

'And so it ought to be,' replied the second, 'for all the money it cost us.'

Jock was at a bitterly fought Rangers *v.* Celtic football match in Glasgow. The man next to him was terrified as the missiles flew over their heads.

'Don't worry,' Jock assured him, 'you won't get hit by a bottle unless it's got your name on it.'

'That's what I'm afraid of,' said the man, lowering his head further. 'My name is Johnny Walker.'

* * *

A man lost fifty pence this morning in the high street,' said McTavish to a friend, 'and I couldn't move until the crowd dispersed.'

'Why couldn't you move?' asked the friend.

'Well,' said McTavish, 'I didn't want to take my foot off the fifty pence piece.'

* * *

Jock was only five feet tall. He attributed his lack of height to the fact that as a lad in Scotland he was fed exclusively on condensed milk and shortbread.

* * *

McNab was once arrested by the police for breaking into a five pound note.

However, he was let off with a caution as it was his first offence.

McNab sat on the side of his bed one Sunday morning solemnly contemplating some money which he had taken from the pocket of his weekday trousers.

'Now let me see,' he said to himself. 'When I went out on the spree with those three Englishmen, I had a fifty pence piece, a tenpenny piece and a fivepenny piece. Now I've only got the fifty pence piece and the tenpenny piece. What on earth did I do with the five pence?'

* * *

What does a Scottish breakfast consist of?

A pound of steak, a bottle of whisky and a large Alsatian dog. The dog is to eat the steak.

* * *

Each true Scotsman yearns
For the land of Burns.
But a major snag is
The confounded haggis.

* * *

Jock was unemployed for many years and had given up hope of ever finding a job. He almost lived in his local pub and his lack of income forced him to cadge drinks from all the regulars.

He continued to attend interview after interview but with his advancing years his chances dwin-

dled. Then he had a stroke of good luck – the Gas Board offered him a temporary job collecting money from meters. He prepared for the job with great care and attention and read all the literature he could find before he set off to work on Monday morning. On Monday night he was back in his local pub feeling on top of the world and buying glasses of whisky for everyone in the pub.

'This is terrific,' shouted a friend to him across the din. 'I suppose it will be doubles all round when you get paid on Friday.'

'What?' said Jock. 'Do I get paid as well?'

* * *

Doctor: 'I think we can just about save your life, sir, but it will take an operation that will cost about a thousand pounds.'

McTavish: 'That's a terrible extravagance, doctor – do you think it's worth it?'

* * *

What is the definition of an atheist?

Someone who goes to a Glasgow Rangers *v.* Glasgow Celtic match to watch the football.

* * *

McTavish bought his wife an expensive Japanese fan.

He told her it would last for years if she held it still and moved her head from side to side.

McNab opened a little tea shop and McTavish asked him how it was going.

'Grand,' said McNab. 'We had our first customer the other day but unfortunately the kettle wasn't boiling.'

* * *

Sir Harry Lauder, one of Scotland's most famous sons, was once interviewed by a reporter who asked him how he had managed to amass such a large fortune.

'Well, it's a long story,' he replied, 'and since we have no need for light while I'm telling it, let me blow out the candle.'

'I don't think you need to tell me any more,' said the reporter.

* * *

MacPherson bought a brand new mousetrap but when he got home he was annoyed to find that he had no cheese left. He had the brainwave of cutting out a very realistic-looking picture of a piece of cheese from a magazine and putting it in the trap. Next morning he examined the trap and found it contained a very realistic-looking picture of a mouse.

* * *

Much may be made of a Scotsman, if he is caught young.

Samuel Johnson

Jock was at the zoo when he fell into a huge tank containing half a dozen man-eating sharks. However, he lived to tell the tale because he was wearing a T-shirt which said: SCOTLAND FOR THE WORLD CUP.

Not even the sharks would swallow that!

* * *

Have you heard about the Scottish football captain who lent the referee a penny to toss for ends and demanded his whistle as security?

* * *

Jock arrived at the home of his minister at midnight. He was in more than a mild state of intoxication (and so was Jock!).

'Reverend,' he said to him, 'I'm worried about the doctrine of predestination.'

'Look,' said the minister, 'why not come back in the morning when you are in a better condition to discuss theological matters?'

'No,' said Jock. 'When I'm sober, I don't care a damn about predestination.'

* * *

It would require a surgical operation to get a joke into a Scottish understanding.

Rev. Sydney Smith

Jock and Sandy were travelling to Rome to support Glasgow Rangers in the final of the European Cup. Sandy, who had means, was travelling by air, while Jock was travelling overland.

'Where will we meet?' asked Jock.

'Let's meet in the Vatican,' said Sandy.

'In the bar or the lounge?' asked Jock.

* * *

The undertaker called on the ninety-year-old McNab and asked him if he would like to make any arrangements for when he passed away.

'I don't think so,' said the cautious McNab. 'After all, I could be lost at sea.'

* * *

McTavish and McNab visited the Royal Highland Show. During their visit to the bar tent they bought some raffle tickets from the barman. Later, McTavish was delighted when he won the booby prize, which was a toilet brush. He had never won anything before and admired it all the way home on the bus. A few weeks later the two met again and McNab asked McTavish how he was getting on with his toilet brush. 'Well, I didn't think much of it,' confessed McTavish, 'so I'm back to using toilet paper again.'

McNab's wife was in the habit of receiving his pay packet unopened every week. For three weeks in a row, however, she was disturbed to find that the pay packet had been opened and was ten pence short.

Finally she could stand it no longer. 'Look me in the eye,' she ordered him, 'and tell me the name of this other woman you've been taking out.'

* * *

Have your heard about the Scotsman who told his little boy that the gas meter was a savings bank?

* * *

McDougal was sentenced to death by hanging. On hearing that it would cost £200 to have him executed in this manner, he said to the authorities, 'Look, give me twenty-five pounds and I'll shoot myself.'

* * *

Jock and his wife came out of the cinema one night and he said to her, 'Would you like to walk or take a taxi?'

'Let's take a taxi, Jock,' she replied. 'Don't be so Jewish.'

The old railway line from Inverness to Aberdeen was never renowned for luxury and comfort. A story is told of an old colonel who was heard to remark when he arrived in Aberdeen on that train, 'Well, thank the Lord, that's the worst part of the journey over.'

'What is your destination?' asked a fellow passenger.

'Bangkok,' replied the colonel.

* * *

Jock was playing golf with an elder of the kirk. On the last hole he missed a six-inch putt which cost him the match but, out of deference to his playing partner's status, he said absolutely nothing.

'That,' said the elder, 'was the most profane silence I have ever heard.'

* * *

McDougal decided to repair the roof of his four-storey house in order to save the expense of hiring a workman. However, when he was only half-way through the job he slipped and fell off the roof. Passing by the kitchen window on his plunge downwards, he shouted to his wife, 'No dinner for me today!'

Why are Scotsmen so good at golf?

They realize that the fewer times they hit the ball the longer it will last.

* * *

'Why are you crying, little man?' a kindly old lady asked McTavish's little boy.

'Because I lost ten pence,' he howled.

'Don't cry,' she said. 'There's ten pence for you.'

Young McTavish took the money and howled even louder.

'What's the matter now?' she asked him.

'If I hadn't lost the first ten pence,' he wailed, 'I'd have twenty pence now.'

* * *

Two Glasgow women were talking. 'How is your married daughter Kirsty getting on?' asked one.

'Fine, just fine,' answered the other. 'A fine house, a fur coat, and two cars. There's just one thing wrong – she can't stand her husband.'

'Aye,' said the first, 'there's always something.'

* * *

Have you heard about the Scotsman who was suffering from alcoholic constipation?

He couldn't pass a pub.

McNab was stopped by a beggar who asked him for some money. 'I haven't eaten for over three days,' he added sadly.

'What self-control,' marvelled McNab. 'Go on, force yourself.'

* * *

I have been trying all my life to like Scotsmen and am obliged to desist from the experiment in despair.

Charles Lamb

* * *

'I hear McDougal left over a hundred thousand pounds when he died,' remarked McNab.

'McDougal didn't leave that money,' said McTavish, 'he was taken from it.'

* * *

McTavish became depressed and decided to end it all by hanging himself. However, his friend McNab came along in the nick of time, cut the rope and saved McTavish's life.

McTavish, true to form, sent him a bill for the cost of the rope.

McNab was travelling by train to London so he handed in a twenty pound note and asked for a ticket.

The clerk said, 'Certainly, sir. By the way, change at Crewe.'

'I'll have mine now, if you don't mind,' said McNab.

* * *

There are few more impressive sights in the world than a Scotsman on the make.

James Barrie

* * *

McTavish and McNab were mountaineering in the French Alps when McTavish slipped and fell into a crevice.

'Run quickly down to the village,' he shouted to McNab, 'and get a rope – I'll try to hang on by my fingernails until you get back.'

After about an hour McNab reappeared.

'Well, have you got the rope?' McTavish shouted.

'No,' said McNab, 'those skinflints in the village wanted two pounds for it.'

Jock, feeling full of religious fervour and Scotch whisky, hurled a bottle of Domestos through the window of his local church.

He was fined for bleach of the priest.

* * *

'Why, McTavish,' said the psychiatrist, 'you seem to have lost your stutter.'

'Yes,' said McTavish, 'I've been telephoning America a lot recently.'

* * *

Every week four Scotsmen got together to drink a bottle of whisky. One night, after many years of meeting, Jock said, 'I got some bad news today: I'm not long for this world, but when I pass on I'd like to think that when you meet you all keep me a dram and pour it over my grave.'

After a moment's silence one of the others asked, 'Would it not be better, Jock, if we gave it a swill round our kidneys first?'

* * *

'You've woken me up at three in the morning,' said the infuriated chemist, 'just for ten pence worth of bicarbonate of soda, when a glass of hot water would have done just as well.'

'Thank you for your advice,' said McNab. 'I won't bother you after all.'

Have you heard about the Scotsman who never smoked cigarettes with his gloves on?

He hated the smell of burning leather.

* * *

Have you heard about the Scotsman who threw caution to the winds?

He gave the canary another seed.

* * *

McNab was the sort of man who wouldn't tell you the time if he had two watches.

McDougal was the sort of man who wouldn't give you a slide if he owned the Alps.

McTavish was the sort of man who wouldn't give you a light if his trousers were on fire.

* * *

Jock's wife awoke one night to hear her husband stealing about the bedroom in the dark, knocking the furniture over.

'What are you looking for?' she asked him.

'Nothing,' he replied gruffly.

'Then you'll find it in the whisky bottle,' she said, turning over and going back to sleep.

McNab has decided to have one of those cut-price self-service funerals.

They just loosen the earth and you sink in by yourself.

* * *

McTavish was short of cash so he phoned up his friend, McNab, and asked for the loan of ten pounds.

'Sorry,' said McNab, 'you'll have to speak up, I can't hear a word you're saying.'

'Can you lend me ten pounds?' screamed McTavish into the phone.

'Look,' said McNab, 'the line is terrible, I can't make out what you're saying.'

At this stage the operator chipped in and said, 'There's nothing wrong with the line, I can hear the caller distinctly.'

'In that case, why don't you lend him the ten pounds?' retorted McNab.

* * *

McNab wanted to marry McTavish's daughter but couldn't pluck up the courage to propose. Finally he hit on a plan.

'How would you like,' he asked McTavish, 'to find a sure fire way of saving some money?'

Jock McTavish was sitting by the fire one evening when his little son rushed in to tell him there was a strange cow in the garden.

'What will I do with her?' he asked.

'What a silly question,' said Jock. 'Milk her and turn her out.'

* * *

Jock was a great supporter of Glasgow Rangers and never missed an opportunity to watch them play. When they were drawn against Lisbon in Portugal he saved every penny he could lay his hands on for the charter flight in order to support his heroes. He flew out to the match and was heart-broken when Rangers lost 2–1 as the result of a disputed last-minute penalty. Jock decided to drown his sorrows and for three days he drank port wine until all his money had gone. Then he realized his predicament: his charter flight had long since returned home and he had no money to pay the surcharge for a scheduled flight. In desperation he decided to hitch a lift home from one of the many lorry drivers who ply the Iberian Peninsula. For several hours he stood on the road outside Lisbon – a forlorn figure in his kilt and tam-o-shanter. Finally his patience was rewarded when a Scottish lorry driver pulled up and said, 'Hop in lad, and I'll take you to Edinburgh.'

'No good to me,' replied Jock sadly. 'I'm bound for Glasgow.'

McTavish, the Scottish angler, died and was met at the Golden Gates by St Peter.

'You've told too many lies to get in here,' said St Peter.

'Have a heart,' replied McTavish, 'you were a fisherman once yourself.'

* * *

McNab was taking a taxi to the railway station.

'How much will it cost?' he asked the driver.

'Three pounds,' said the driver.

'How much for my suitcase?' asked McNab.

'That goes absolutely free, sir,' said the driver.

'Here, take my case. I'll walk to the station,' said McNab.

* * *

A Scotsman won first prize in a raffle and was offered his choice of a felt hat or a straw hat.

'I'll take the straw hat,' he declared. 'It will be a mouthful for the cow when I'm finished with it.'

* * *

A Scotsman and therefore an expert dram drinker was asked what he thought of Irish whiskey.

'It's useful stuff,' he replied, 'if you run short of water for diluting a Scotch whisky.'

A teacher asked Wee Jock, 'If you had a pound in your right-hand trouser pocket, and three pounds in your left-hand trouser pocket, what would you have?'

Wee Jock replied, 'Somebody else's trousers!'

* * *

Angus McGregor was the first man to swim from New Zealand to Australia. Upon arrival on Australian soil he was met by a TV interviewer. 'Strewth, mate,' gasped the Australian, 'how did you get to be such a fantastic swimmer?'

'From the age of two,' replied Angus, 'my father would take me to Loch Lomond, row me into the middle, help me over the side, and then leave me to swim the thirteen miles back to shore.'

'That must have been hard for a two-year-old,' said the admiring Australian.

'Yes,' agreed Angus, 'but the hardest part was fighting my way out of the sack!'

* * *

The following was seen on a poster in Glasgow:

DRINK IS YOUR ENEMY.

Adjacent to this was another poster which said:

LOVE YOUR ENEMY.

A London magazine once organized a competition to discover the most loved painting in the Tate Gallery. Contestants were asked to answer the following question: If the Tate Gallery were on fire and you were allowed to save one painting which one would it be?

First prize went to a Scotsman, who answered, 'The one nearest the door.'

* * *

Chemist's assistant: 'There's a Scotsman in the shop who wants to buy ten pence worth of arsenic to commit suicide. How can I save him?'

Chemist: 'Tell him it will cost twenty pence.'

* * *

McDougal was on his way by train from Aberdeen to Glasgow to undergo a serious heart operation.

He bought a single ticket.

* * *

Grandpa, have you got any teeth?' McTavish's little son inquired of his grandfather.

'No, my child,' he replied.

'Well, hold my bag of sweets while I go and play,' said little McTavish.

Jock received a summons from his bank manager who informed him sternly that his current account was overdrawn to the extent of £500.

'I'm terribly sorry about that,' said Jock. 'Can I give you a cheque?'

* * *

McNab was enjoying a meal in a posh restaurant.

'Waiter,' he called 'I've just dropped a fivepenny piece under the table. If you find it I want it back, but if not you may have it as a tip.'

* * *

McTavish, a millionaire of ninety-three, decided to marry a lovely young girl of eighteen. The preacher however, did not approve.

'I don't believe in marrying for money,' he told the couple.

'Good,' said McTavish. 'In that case I'll not offer you a fee for performing the ceremony.'

* * *

McTavish's little boy was being questioned by the teacher during an arithmetic lesson.

'If you had five pounds,' said the teacher, 'and I asked you for three, how many would you have then?'

'Five,' said young McTavish.

Have you heard about the Scotsman who took his wife's false teeth to work with him every day to stop her eating between meals?

* * *

McNab: 'I hear you were in the superstore when all the lights went out. Did you get anything?'

McTavish: 'I was very unlucky. I was in the piano department at the time.'

* * *

For those of you who have never seen a haggis, it looks just like a football. (Those of you who have never seen a football, go on to the next joke.) It's hard to know whether you should eat it or kick it. If you eat it, you'll wish you had kicked it.

* * *

A Scotsman had just put a pound on a horse and the horse came in at twenty to one. As the bookmaker handed him twenty-one pound coins the Scotsman examined each one of them carefully.

'What's the matter?' the bookmaker asked. 'Don't you trust me?'

'I'm just making sure that the bad one I gave you isn't among them,' said the Scotsman.

It is rumoured that the entire adult population of Glasgow took to the street with glass in hand when it was forecast that there'd be a nip in the air.

* * *

Sandy McNab had a brass band at his wedding.
It was on the bride's finger.

* * *

Sandy McTavish's nephew came to him with a problem.

'I have my choice of two women,' he told him, 'a beautiful penniless young girl whom I love dearly, and a rich old widow whom I can't stand.'

'Marry the girl you love,' said McTavish.

'I will follow your advice,' said the nephew.

'In that case,' said McTavish, 'could you give me the widow's address?'

* * *

The minister poured Jock a minuscule glass of whisky to celebrate the festive season.

'This whisky,' he told Jock, 'is nearly a hundred years old.'

'Is that a fact?' said Jock. 'Mind you, it's very small for its age!'

Doctor: 'I'll examine you for ten pounds.'

McDougal: 'Good luck to you, doctor, and if you can find them I'll let you have one of them.'

* * *

Jock says his wife is a sex object.

Every time he wants sex she says, 'I object.'

* * *

An Englishman, an Irishman and a Scotsman went out for an afternoon on the town. The Englishman spent ten pounds, the Irishman spent five pounds and the Scotsman spent a very enjoyable afternoon indeed.

* * *

A Scotswoman told her husband that she would like to buy a barometer so as to be able to forecast the weather.

'You don't need a barometer, woman,' he told her. 'What do you think the good Lord gave you your rheumatism for?'

As the *Titanic* was sinking it is said that there was a Scotsman rushing round to all the lifeboats shouting frantically, 'Is there anybody who wants to buy a genuine diamond ring for five pounds?'

* * *

Two Scotsmen bought a bottle of whisky for a pound and it was the vilest brew they had ever tasted.

'I'll be very glad,' said one to the other, 'when we've finished this bottle.'

* * *

Have you heard about the Scotsman who sued a football club for damages because he was injured during a big match?

He fell out of the tree he was sitting in.

* * *

Hall porter: (expecting a tip) 'I hope you had a pleasant stay, sir?'

McTavish: 'Yes I did, but I'm afraid I gave all my small change to the chambermaid.'

Hall porter: (indignantly) 'But she told me you gave her nothing!'

McTavish: 'Well, if I gave a bonnie wee lass like her nothing what chance have you got?'

A beggar stopped a Scotsman and asked him for ten pence for a cup of coffee.

'Show me the cup of coffee first,' said the Scotsman.

* * *

Scotsman: 'Could I hire a horse please?'

Clerk: 'Certainly, sir. Any particular kind?'

Scotsman: 'A long one – there are five of us!'

* * *

True Scotsmen hate to see waste, no matter where in the world they see it.

A Scotsman travelling in Egypt said, on seeing the Pyramids, 'What damn fool built those useless things?'

Another remarked that the Niagara Falls were a perfect waste of water and that there was a plumber in Dundee that could fix them in half an hour.

* * *

McDougal had a dog for sale and was offered £500 for it by an American and £100 by an Englishman.

He sold it to the Englishman because he figured it could walk back from London but never swim the Atlantic.

McNab has his doormat hung up in the hall to save the wear and tear.

* * *

What's the difference between a Scotsman and a canoe?

A canoe sometimes tips.

* * *

They say it takes ten Welshmen to outsmart an Irishman, twenty Irishmen to outsmart an Englishman, and a hundred Englishmen to outsmart a Scotsman.

* * *

There is a foolproof method of teaching a Scotsman to swim.

Pin a five pound note to his bathing trunks and throw him in the water.

* * *

Jock was carrying his inebriated companion into a Temperance hotel.

'I'm sorry,' said the clerk, 'you can't bring him in here. This is a Temperance hotel.'

'Don't worry,' said Jock. 'He's far too drunk to notice.'

McTavish's extravagance finally got him into trouble and he was declared bankrupt. On his way to the bankruptcy court, he hired a Rolls-Royce as a taxi, and invited the owner into court as a creditor.

* * *

They finally picked up the Scottish obscene telephone caller.

He kept reversing the charges.

* * *

Jock's brother Hamish had an unusual job.

He used to find things before other people lost them.

* * *

While paying a visit to Dublin, McDougal was amazed by the number of seagulls flying about.

'What do those birds live on?' he asked his guide.

'Scraps of food thrown away,' answered the guide.

'Funny that we have no birds like that in Scotland,' said McDougal.

McDougal donates a lot of money to charity but he likes to remain anonymous.

In fact he doesn't even sign his name on the cheques.

* * *

A Scotsman had a horse and carriage which he used to provide a taxi service from the railway station.

'That's a miserably thin animal,' said a tourist as he slowly mounted the carriage.

'He's the unluckiest horse in the world,' said the Scotsman.

'How do you mean, unlucky?' asked the tourist.

'Well,' said the Scotsman, 'every morning I toss a coin to see whether he gets a feed of oatmeal or I buy myself a glass of whisky. The unfortunate animal has lost for the last six mornings running.'

* * *

McNab has just had his dustbin fitted with a burglar alarm.

* * *

A meeting was held in a Scottish town to protest about the fact that bus fares had been reduced from twenty pence to fifteen pence. Citizens were annoyed because previously they had saved twenty pence by not using the buses whereas now they were saving only fifteen pence.

A Rangers football fan told his friend, 'My dog watches all the games. When my team wins it jumps up and down and claps its paws. When we lose it turns somersaults.'

'How many somersaults?' asked his friend, impressed.

The Rangers fan replied, 'It depends how hard I kick it!'

* * *

Jock was travelling to Glasgow by train and when it stopped at a small station a man came out with a little hammer and tapped all the wheels.

'Why are you doing that?' Jock asked him.

'I've been doing it for twenty-five years,' said the man, 'and I haven't the foggiest notion.'

* * *

A Scotsman went on a week's holiday to London taking with him a shirt and a five pound note. When he arrived home he hadn't changed either of them!

* * *

A man called at Jock's door one evening collecting for the Home for Chronic Alcoholics.

Jock's wife answered the door. 'Call back after closing time,' she told the man, 'and you can have my husband.'

McTavish suffered a brainstorm and bought two tenpenny tickets in a raffle. He won £1000.

'How do you feel about your big win?' McNab asked him.

'Disappointed,' said McTavish. 'My other ticket didn't win anything.'

* * *

McDougal walked into a fish and chip shop.

'I want ten pence worth of chips please,' he said. 'I want lots of salt and vinegar on them, two pence worth of pickled onions, and wrap the whole lot in today's newspaper.'

* * *

A little girl asked an elderly Scotsman for a contribution to a religious organization – 'money for the Lord' as she put it.

'How old are you, wee lassie?' he asked her.

'Ten years old,' she replied.

'Well, I'm eighty,' he said. 'I'm bound to see the Lord before you do and I'll give him the money myself.'

* * *

Recent historical research has shown why Scotsmen wear kilts.

In 1317 Sandy McNab won a lady's tartan skirt in a raffle.

The Scots have an infallible cure for sea-sickness.

You lean over the side of the ship with a ten pence piece in your mouth.

* * *

There was a terrible row at a Glasgow cinema the other evening. Two Scotsmen were trying to get in on the same ticket on the grounds that they were half-brothers.

* * *

'Where do you come from?' Jock asked an American.

'From the greatest country in the world,' replied the American.

'Well,' said Jock, 'you've got the queerest Scottish accent I've ever heard.'

* * *

On Monday morning a Scottish shopkeeper was surprised to have two toilet rolls returned with the following note:

> Could you please refund my money on these toilet rolls? Uncle Douglas and Aunt Mary didn't come for the weekend after all!

McNab gave up reading the free newspapers at the public library because of the wear and tear on his glasses.

* * *

Have you heard about the least disturbed mouse in Scotland?

He lives in the offertory box of an Aberdeen church.

* * *

McDougal kept vigil at the bedside of his dying wife for several days. Finally he said, 'Agnes, I must go away on business now, but I'll hurry back. If you feel yourself slipping away while I'm gone, would you mind blowing out the candle?'

* * *

McTavish was walking one day on the golf course when he was struck on the head by a golf ball. Angrily, he demanded £500 compensation from the golfer who had driven the shot.

'But I said "fore",' said the golfer.

'Done,' said McTavish.

* * *

The Scotsman's dilemma: Whether to take longer steps to save shoe leather or shorter steps to avoid the strain on the stitches of his underpants.

Jock McTavish was due for a medical examination. As requested by the doctor, he took along a generous specimen in a large bottle. After the test the doctor said, 'You're fine. I couldn't find a thing wrong with you.'

Jock happily returned home and announced to his wife, 'Good news, Mary. You and I and the kids and Uncle Sandy are all in perfect shape.'

* * *

Jock, McTavish and McNab were neighbours and all were keen beekeepers. It annoyed McTavish and McNab that every year Jock would win the local best honey competition. Jock always maintained he had a secret which helped him win. One night McTavish got Jock drunk and extracted the secret from him. He raced round to tell McNab, 'I've found out Jock's great secret; every morning he lets his bees out at five o'clock so they can go down to the park and get the earliest and best pollen.'

'He's a liar,' roared McNab, 'the park gates don't open till nine!'

* * *

McTavish took his girlfriend out in a hired boat on the loch. It started to rain and finally it came down so hard that McTavish said, 'We're getting drenched. I wish the hour was up so we could row ashore.'

The nervous candidate was being interviewed by the elders of the kirk to see if he was suitable to become their new minister.

'Are you a paper preacher?' they asked him.

'What on earth is a paper preacher?' he asked in dismay.

'If you write your sermons down on paper,' said one of the elders, 'then we know you will finish when there's no more paper. But if you don't, God only knows when you will finish.'

* * *

The great Scottish poet William McGonagall was heard to remark, 'Burns is dead, Sir Walter Scott is dead, and I'm not feeling too well myself.'

* * *

There was a Scottish baker who tried to economize by making a bigger hole in his doughnuts. He discovered that the bigger the hole he made, the more dough it took to go round it.

* * *

'What made you suspect that these two men were drunk, officer?' a Glasgow magistrate asked a policeman in court.

'Well, Your Honour,' said the policeman, 'Jock was throwing five pound notes away and Sandy kept picking them up and handing them back to him.'

McDougal heard about a doctor who charged ten pounds for the first consultation but only three pounds for every subsequent visit. So he waltzed into the doctor's surgery and announced, 'Here I am again, Doc.'

'Keep up the treatment I prescribed last time,' said the doctor, who was also a Scotsman.

* * *

A pilot friend decided to take Jock and Maggie for a trip in his light aeroplane. However, he hated talk and conversation and told his passengers they would be charged ten pounds if either of them spoke, but not charged otherwise.

They had a wonderful trip with loops, dives and every trick the pilot knew. Not a word was spoken, so when they landed the pilot said to Jock, 'That was wonderful, not a word. Tell me, were you tempted to speak at all?'

'Only once,' said Jock.

'When was that?' asked the pilot.

'When Maggie fell out!'

* * *

In later years McNab became quite deaf but didn't feel like forking out for a hearing aid. So he bought a long piece of flex, put one end in his breast pocket and the other end in his ear. It didn't improve his hearing very much but he found that people spoke to him a bit more loudly.

Have you heard about the Scotsman whose horse swallowed a ten pence piece?

He's been riding backwards every since.

* * *

Daddy, who is that man running up and down the carriage with his mouth open?'

'Don't worry, son, that's a Scotsman getting a free smoke.'

* * *

Have you heard about the Scotsman who married a girl born on 29 February?

He had to buy her a birthday present only once every four years.

* * *

A Scotsman lay dying in London so they sent word to his relatives in Aberdeen to come at once. His brother cycled all the way from Scotland to London. When he arrived he took the bicycle into the sick man's bedroom and released all the air from the tyres. Within a few minutes his brother had recovered completely.

The one thing that annoyed Wee Jock's friends about him was that no matter who they were talking about, Wee Jock always said he knew them. One night they were talking about Barry Manilow's forthcoming tour, and sure enough, Wee Jock told them that he knew Barry. His friends bought tickets for the show and afterwards, backstage, they met Barry who hugged Wee Jock and then invited him into his dressing room for a drink.

Some time later, talk got round to a meeting Neil Kinnock was holding and, once again, Wee Jock claimed he knew Neil. On the night of the meeting they all attended, and when Neil caught sight of Wee Jock he left the platform and embraced him warmly.

A few weeks later, talk got round to the Duke of Edinburgh, and once again Wee Jock claimed he knew him. Determined to call his bluff, the friends all went down to London. On reaching Buck House they were told that only one could gain admittance. Wee Jock said, 'Look, I'll go inside and bring the Duke out to that balcony over there.'

He left, and quarter of an hour later two figures appeared on the balcony. The friends couldn't make out who the figure with Wee Jock was. 'Excuse us,' said one of the group to a passing tourist, 'could you tell us if that tall man up there is the Duke of Edinburgh?'

The tourist looked up and said, 'I don't know if the tall guy is the Duke of Edinburgh, but the little one is Wee Jock!'

An Englishman, an Irishman and a Scotsman went into a pub. The Englishman stood a round, the Irishman stood a round and the Scotsman stood around.

* * *

A Scotsman took a girl for a taxi ride. She was so beautiful he could hardly keep his eyes on the meter.

* * *

A company sent a politely worded reminder to a Scotsman that his account was long overdue. They received the following reply:

> Dear Sir,
>
> I divide my creditors into three groups: (i) Those paid at once (ii) Those paid sometimes (iii) Those never paid.
>
> I am happy to inform you that because of the friendly tone of your letter you have been promoted from group (iii) to group (ii).
>
> Yours faithfully,
> Jock Murphy

* * *

A Scottish obituary: 'This man is gone to where he can light his pipe with his finger.'

A Scotsman on holiday in Iraq was giving directions to a friend on how to get to his hotel.

'The hotel is situated,' he told him, 'about ten miles on the Glasgow side of Baghdad.'

* * *

McTavish went into a shop to buy a suitcase.

'Shall I wrap it for you, sir?' asked the assistant.

'No,' said McTavish, 'just put the string and paper inside.'

* * *

McDougal found a bottle of cough mixture so he sent his children out to play in their pyjamas in the snow.

* * *

The Scottish minister was preaching on the parable of the Good Samaritan. He felt he had better explain to his congregation why the priest had passed the victim by.

'And why do you think the priest passed him by?' he asked them rhetorically.

'Because he saw that the man had already been robbed,' came a voice from the back of the hall.

McDougal took his girlfriend out for an evening and they were back at the door of her flat just before midnight. As she kissed him goodnight she said, 'Be careful on your way home now, darling. I'd hate anyone to rob you of all the money you've saved this evening.'

* * *

While shopping in Scotland an Englishman bought an article, placed a five pound note on the counter and went out without his change. The shopkeeper tried frantically to attract his attention by knocking on the window with a sponge.

* * *

A Scotsman went to church and by mistake put fifty pence in the collection plate. He asked the minister if he could have it back but was told that was impossible. For the next forty-nine Sundays, when the plate was placed in front of him he passed it on saying, 'Season.'

* * *

Have you heard about the Scotsman who murdered both his parents so he could go on the orphans' picnic?

In some Scottish restaurants they heat the knives so you can't use too much butter.

* * *

They've stopped the crime wave in Scotland by putting a sign over the the jailhouse saying:

> ANYBODY CONVICTED AND PUT IN JAIL WILL HAVE TO PAY FOR HIS BOARD AND LODGING.

* * *

A Scotsman decided to give up pipe smoking for the following reasons:

1. When he used his own tobacco he never used enough to get a decent smoke.
2. When he smoked someone else's his pipe was always packed so tight he could never light it.

* * *

McNab had counted his change four times at a shop counter.

'What's the matter?' asked the assistant. 'Haven't I given you enough change?'

'Yes,' said McNab, 'but only just.'

* * *

In Scotland they had to take pay-as-you-leave buses off the streets – they found two men had starved to death in one of them.

A Scottish doctor was asked by a friend what treatment he would prescribe for a patient with a cold.

'Give him a glass of whisky,' said the doctor, 'and send him to bed.'

'Suppose he had a severe cold in his chest,' said the friend.

'Give him two glasses of whisky,' said the doctor, 'and send him to bed.'

'Suppose the treatment hadn't worked after a week,' said the friend. 'What then?'

'Give him four glasses of whisky,' said the doctor, 'and send him to bed.'

'But,' said the friend in desperation, 'suppose the treatment hadn't worked after a month.'

'Give him eight glasses of whisky,' said the doctor, 'and send him to bed.'

The friend tried a different line of attack. 'What if the patient didn't drink whisky?' he asked.

'Then,' said the Scottish doctor with a twinkle in his eye, 'he's nae worth curing.'

* * *

A lodger in a Scottish guest house was on his way to the bathroom when the landlady stopped him and said, 'Have you got a good memory for faces?'

'Yes,' he replied.

'That's just as well,' she said, 'because there's no mirror in the bathroom.'

McDougal found a pair of crutches in the attic, so he went downstairs and broke his wife's leg.

* * *

McNab's wife had a temperature of 105°F.

So he put her in the cellar to heat the house.

* * *

Hamish told Jock that he had found a foolproof way of making money. 'I take a hundred pounds,' he said, 'and have it changed into twenty five pound notes. Then take each five pound note and have it changed into five one pound coins. Then I take each one pound coin and have it changed into a hundred pennies. Then I take all the pennies back to the bank and have them changed back into a hundred pound note.'

The bewildered Jock asked, 'How on earth do you make money that way?'

'Well,' replied Hamish, 'every so often somebody makes a mistake and I just make sure it's not me.'

* * *

A Scottish salesman died while travelling for his company in the Highlands.

His manager sent the following telegram:

RETURN SAMPLES BY FREIGHT. SEARCH POCKETS FOR ORDERS.

An old Scottish doctor was called out at two o'clock one morning through snowdrifts and blizzards to assist at a birth. As he crawled back into bed at six, his wife said to him, 'A doctor's life is a very hard one.'

'Aye, lass,' he agreed, 'but a very rewarding one. Guess who was born this morning? Robbie Burns.'

* * *

Two robbers attacked a boarding house in Glasgow in search of money, and a fierce struggle resulted.

'We didn't do too badly,' said one as they counted the loot. 'We got twenty pounds between us.'

'But we had thirty before we went in,' wailed the other.

* * *

McDougal has developed a nice little racket. Whenever he and his wife go out for an evening, they get their kids to do a song-and-dance act for the baby sitter and deduct a cover charge from her money.

* * *

McNab was once run over by a brewery lorry.

It was the first time for years that the drinks had been on him.

You've heard of Irish coffee, but have you tried Scottish coffee?

It's hot water flavoured with burnt toast.

* * *

McDougal walked into a shop and asked for a cheap coat-hanger.

'Certainly sir,' said the shop assistant. 'Here's a nice one for five pence.'

'Don't you have anything cheaper?' asked McDougal.

'Yes, sir, a nail,' said the disgusted assistant.

* * *

'I was so sorry to hear that your wife died,' Sandy sympathized with Jock.

'You're not nearly as sorry as I am,' replied Jock. 'She had taken hardly any of those expensive pills I'd bought her.'

* * *

McDougal joined a hunting party in Canada. After a time a large animal was sighted.

'What's that?' asked McDougal.

'That's a Canadian moose,' he was told.

'Well, I'd hate to see a Canadian rat,' he replied.

How do you disperse an angry Scottish mob?

Take up a collection.

* * *

Jock's tooth was paining him so he decided to visit the dentist. As he sat nervously in the dentist's chair he fumbled in his pocket.

'There's no need to pay me in advance,' said the dentist.

'It's not that at all,' replied Jock. 'I'm just counting my money before you put me under gas.'

* * *

A Scottish piper was asked what was the purpose of the drones in his bagpipes, in view of the distressing sound they made.

'Without the drones,' he replied, 'you might as well be playing the piano.'

* * *

Hamish was so much troubled with his tooth that he decided to have it extracted.

'How much will it cost?' he asked the dentist.

'Three pounds,' replied the dentist.

'Isn't that a lot for a few minutes' work?' said Hamish.

'Well, I can pull it slowly if you like,' said the dentist.

'Look,' said Hamish, 'here's one pound. Just loosen it a bit.'

Sex expert Professor McNab was touring Scotland and his theme was 'Make love often – and be happier.' At the close of his meeting he asked the audience to help him. 'Will all those couples who make love more than once a week, please stand up?' Three quarters of the assembled stood up, all wearing happy smiles.

'That's proved my point,' said the Professor, 'now will those couples who only make love once a month please stand up.' A few couples stood up, not looking nearly as happy as the first group.

'Not as happy as the previous lot,' said the Professor. 'Now, is there any couple who only make love once a year?' To this request only one couple stood up, with huge smiles wreathed across their faces.

'I did ask,' said the surprised Professor, 'for couples who only make love once a year.'

'That's right,' replied the smiling man, 'we only make love once a year.'

'But how can you be so happy?' queried the shaken Professor.

The couple's smiles widened even more when the man replied, 'Tonight's the night!'

* * *

Did you hear about the very generous Scotsman?

He offered £25,000 to the first person to swim the Atlantic.

McTavish and McNab were out walking on a lonely road when suddenly they were held up by a mugger.

'Hand over all your money at once,' he ordered.

'Here's that fifty pounds I owe you,' said McTavish to McNab.

* * *

This fellow went to a Scottish doctor and said, 'Doc, I've got a very poor memory. What do you advise?'

'Well, you can pay me in advance for one thing.'

* * *

A Scotsman living in London was always boasting about his native land to his English friends.

'Why didn't you stay in Scotland,' one of them asked him, 'if it's such a wonderful place?'

'Well,' he explained, 'they were much too clever for me there, but I get on quite well here.'

* * *

Sandy and Jock dined together and after the meal Jock was heard to call for the bill for both of them. Next day the newspapers carried the headline: Ventriloquist found murdered.

McDougal had a fish and chip shop opposite the bank. Late one night a fellow came in and said, 'Could you possibly lend me five pounds. I'm really stuck.'

'Sorry,' said McDougal, 'I couldn't possibly do that because of an arrangement I've got with the bank.'

'What arrangement is that?' asked the fellow.

'They don't sell fish and chips and I don't lend money.'

* * *

An Englishman, an Irishman and a Scotsman were each left £5000 by a rich man on condition that after his death each put twenty pounds in his coffin in case he needed it in the afterlife. The Englishman put in ten pounds, the Irishman put in ten pounds and the Scotsman took out the twenty pounds and put in a cheque for thirty.

* * *

A sales rep boarded the London–Edinburgh sleeper and immediately went to find the sleeping car attendant. He impressed upon the attendant the importance of him being in Berwick in the morning, and told him no matter how fast asleep he was to kick him off the train if necessary. In the morning the sales rep found himself in Edinburgh. He went to find the attendant once more and the language he used was bluer than a Rangers shirt.

When he finally stormed off, an elderly gentleman near by exclaimed, 'I've never heard such foul language in my life before.'

'Oh, that's nothing,' said the attendant, 'you should've heard the man I threw off at Berwick!'

* * *

No collection of Scottish jokes would be complete without the following report from a Glasgow newspaper: 'Two taxis collided in Maryhill last night. Three people were seriously injured. The other seventeen escaped with cuts and bruises.'

* * *

McDougal was anxiously searching his pockets.

'What's the matter?' asked a friend.

'I've lost a five pound note,' said McDougal, 'and I've searched every pocket except one.'

'Why don't you search that pocket?' asked the friend.

'Because if it's not there,' said McDougal, 'I'll drop down dead.'

* * *

At an auction in Glasgow a wealthy American lost a wallet containing over £10,000. He made an announcement about his loss and added that he would give £100 to the finder.

From the back a clearly Scottish accent shouted, 'I'll give a hundred and fifty.'

McTavish was travelling by rail in America. He asked the railway clerk for a ticket to Springfield.

'Which Springfield, mister?' asked the clerk. 'Missouri, Ohio, Illinois or Massachusetts?'

'Which is cheapest?' asked McTavish.

* * *

Jock's mother Flora was the sort of woman who had a good word for everybody, no matter how bad or evil.

'How about Ould Nick himself,' asked Jock. 'Surely you haven't anything good to say about him?'

'Well,' said Flora, 'you've got to admit that the Devil is an industrious wee spirit.'

* * *

McTavish was taking his girlfriend for a drive on his motorbike. As they passed a hot dog stand she sighed, 'My, those hot dogs smell nice.'

'Hold on a moment,' said McTavish gallantly. 'I'll drive a little closer so you can get a better smell.'

* * *

Stand behind your lover, woman,' shouted the Scotsman who had come home and surprised his wife with another man. 'I'm going to shoot you both.'

It is now not generally believed that golf originated in Scotland.

No Scotsman would invent a game in which it was possible to lose a ball.

* * *

An elder of the kirk was surprised and disgusted to see Jock staggering out of his local boozer one night.

'Jock, Jock,' he chided him, 'and I always thought you were a teetotaller.'

'Yes I am, elder,' said Jock, 'but not a bigoted one.'

* * *

McNab: 'Could you led me a tenner?'

McTavish: 'I will when I get paid.'

McNab: 'When will that be?'

McTavish: 'When I start working.'

* * *

Have you heard the one about the Scotsman who gave an Englishman, a Welshman and an Irishman a present of twenty pounds each?

Neither has anyone else.

Mrs McDougal went out and lost her handbag containing all her jewellery and a beautiful pearl necklace given to her by her husband as a birthday present.

McDougal commented, 'It's not so much the loss of the jewellery I mind, but there was a fifty pence piece in the handbag.'

* * *

Just after McTavish had got married he said to the minister, 'I'm sorry I have no money to pay the fees due to you, but if you take me down to your cellar, I'll show you how to fix your gas meter so that it won't register.'

* * *

McNab will never forget the time he spilled a bottle of whisky on the floor by mistake.

He still has splinters in his mouth.

* * *

Jock had a pet dog so he decided to call it by a biblical name. He chose the name 'Moreover' because he remembered the biblical verse: 'Moreover, the dog came and licked his sores.'

Scottish football referees do pretty well financially.

They get five pence back on every bottle.

* * *

Sign in a Scottish garage:

THE MAN WHO LENDS TOOLS IS OUT

* * *

A tramp decided he would shame McDougal into giving him some money, so he went on his hands and knees and began to eat the grass in McDougal's front garden.

McDougal stuck his head out the window and asked him what he was doing.

'I'm eating the grass,' said the tramp, 'because I'm starving.'

'Come on in,' said McDougal, 'and I'll let you into my back garden. The grass is much longer there.'

* * *

A minister during a church service noticed that the collection plate consisted of lots of pound coins and three pennies.

'I see we must have a Scotsman in the congregation,' he said jokingly at the beginning of his sermon.

A Scotsman at the back of the church stood up, and said, 'Your Reverence, there are three of us.'

It had been a bitterly cold day on the Scottish golf course and the caddie was expecting a handsome tip from his rich Scottish client.

As they approached the clubhouse the caddie heard the magic words, 'This is for a hot glass of whisky.' So he held out his hand and received a lump of sugar.

* * *

McTavish took a trip to London but returned the very next day.

'Why did you return so soon?' asked McNab.

'I couldn't stand the extravagance of the place,' said McTavish, 'I hadn't been there more than three hours, when bang went fifty pence.'

'Go on,' said McNab, 'what did you spend it on?'

'I don't rightly remember,' said McTavish, 'but it was mostly wine and women.'

* * *

An old Scotsman was watching a game of golf for the first time.

'What do you think of it?' asked a friend.

'It looks to me,' was the reply, 'like a harmless little ball chased by men too old to chase anything else.'

A salesman was trying to sell a suit to McNab.

'Remember, sir,' he told him, 'there's an extra pair of trousers with this suit.'

'Throw in an extra jacket and it's a deal,' said McNab.

* * *

McDougal was working for a farmer who asked him if he would like to be paid in advance or on completion of the job.

'I'll have the money now, if you don't mind,' said McDougal. 'There's been a lot of sudden deaths recently.'

* * *

How do you recognize a left-handed Scotsman?

He keeps all his money in his right-hand pocket.

* * *

Have you heard about the lecherous McTavish who lured a maiden up to his attic to see his etchings?

He sold her four of them.

The following advertisement appeared in a Scottish newspaper: 'A gentleman who has lost a left leg would like to correspond with another who has lost his right leg and takes a size nine shoe.'

* * *

McDougal received £10,000 for injuries received in a traffic accident while his wife received £2000.

'How badly injured was your wife?' a friend asked.

'Oh, my wife wasn't injured in the accident at all,' replied McDougal, 'but I had the presence of mind to kick her in the teeth before the police arrived.'

* * *

The minister was the only person in the village not to have been booked by the zealous traffic warden. One day the warden jumped out on to the pedestrian crossing as the minister cycled down the road, holding up a hand right in front of the minister, who screeched to a halt. The warden shouted, 'I'll get you for something yet.'

'The Lord is with me still,' replied the minister.

'That's it – two on a bike!' said the warden. And booked him.

McDougal asked a bus conductor how much the bus fare into the city was.

'Fifteen pence,' said the conductor.

McDougal thought this was a bit much so he decided to run behind the bus for a few stops.

'How much is the fare now?' he panted, after running three stops behind the bus.

'Still fifteen pence,' said the conductor.

McDougal ran three further stops behind the bus and could just about manage to ask the conductor again what the fare was now.

'Twenty pence,' said the conductor. 'You're running in the wrong direction.'

* * *

A Scottish proverb: Never drink whisky with water and never drink water without whisky.

* * *

What's the difference between a tightrope and a Scotsman?

A tightrope sometimes gives.

* * *

Jock attended the Temperance lecture given by one of the country's top medical men who was also a noted anti-drink campaigner. The speaker commenced by taking a live worm, all wriggling and moving, and placing it in a large container of whisky. After a few moments the worm died and sank to the bottom.

The speaker turned to his audience and said quietly, 'Now, my friends, what does this prove to us?'

Jock piped up, 'If you drink whisky, you won't be troubled by worms.'

* * *